D1460428

The Beginner Investor: A Beginner's Guide to Stock Market Investing

The Revised Edition

By Danial Jiwani

ISBN: 9781091781825

Dedication Page

This book is dedicated to John Blix, my high school investments teacher. Mr. Blix, taught me much of the information that I have shared with you in this book: diversification, dividends etcetera. He is an excellent teacher as he is able to pass down practical knowledge in a fun and meaningful way. I hope that he is and will be a successful investor!

Contents

The Definition of a Stock

"Know what you own, and know why you own it."
-Peter Lynch

In order to start investing in stocks, it is important to understand what a stock is. A stock is, at its most basic level, ownership in a company. When an investor buys a stock of a company, he is technically a part owner in that company. So if an investor buys Facebook's stock, he owns a small portion of Facebook. The proportion of an investor's ownership grows with the number of shares[1] he owns. For example, if a company issued 1,000 shares of stock and, if an investor owned 100 shares, or 10% of the shares, it means that he owns 10% of the company. If an investor owns 200 of the 1,000 shares, or 20% of the shares, he owns 20% of the company. However, this does not mean that he is entitled to 20% of the company's profits; an investor cannot go to Facebook's headquarters if he owns their stock and demand for some money. Rather, owning a portion of a company entitles an investor to a portion of the company's dividends. A dividend is a payment that a company's board of directors will make *if* they want to distribute a *portion* of the company's profits to

---

[1] A share is similar to a stock. Like a stock, a share is ownership in a company. However, when someone says that he or she owns shares, it usually refers to a number. For example, an investor would say he owns 20 shares of Apples- not twenty stocks of Apple. If he says he owns 20 stocks, it would refer to twenty different companies.

shareholders. Whenever a company decides to pay a dividend, shareholders are entitled to that money based on the amount of shares they own. The dividends are paid in proportion to the number of shares an investor owns. If you own 25% of a company that pays a dividend of one hundred dollars, you are entitled to $25.

A dividend differs from a profit because dividends are a *portion* of the profit that a company decides to pay out to shareholders[2]; a firm can decide to distribute a *part* of its profits to shareholders. Profit is the revenue (money) a company makes minus its costs (expenses). Usually, profits are reinvested back into the company, used to pay off debts, or distributed to shareholders as dividends. Moreover, a dividend is a profit for the investor, which is distributed from the firm's profits, while a regular profit is for the company; profits are reinvested in the company and a dividend is reinvested in an investor's portfolio.

It is important to recognize that not all companies pay a dividend; if and how much the company pays is determined by what the firm's management desires. They can pay $5 for each share, or one cent. In fact, many companies will decide not to pay a dividend.

We will explore the importance of a dividend when finding a valuable stock, in the chapter called *Dividends*. For now, this is what you need to understand about dividends: when an investor owns a stock, he owns a part

---

[2] A shareholder is an investing term to describe someone who owns shares, or stock in a company.

of the company, and he is entitled to the company's dividends, but not profits.

The Importance of Investing

"How many millionaires do you know who have become wealthy by investing in savings accounts? I rest my case."
　　　- Robert G. Allen

　　　Investing is mathematically one of the most efficient ways to build wealth and gain financial independence. The best way to illustrate this is by looking at the mathematics behind the growth in wealth of someone who saves their money versus someone who invests their money. In the first scenario, Billy, a saver, has $1000 in the bank and he adds $50 each month to his account. He wants to save money for the long term. He is concerned with having as much money as possible when he retires. By the end of 50 years, he would have saved… $31,000. In order to calculate this, we used a linear expression.
Accumulated Wealth = (12 * 50 * 50) + 1000
What if Billy had invested? If he was the average investor, seeing his portfolio[3] increase in value by 8% per year after inflation, he would have over $400,000 by the end of 50 years. In order to get this value, we used a compound interest calculator. If you search "compound interest calculator" on Google, you will find many sites that are similar to the one I used. It will show you how much money you can make if you invested for 10 years, 20 years,

---

[3] The word portfolio refers to the collection of stocks and other assets a person owns.

100 years, or if you made, on average, 2%, 5% or 12%, per year. But the point is, the total money you can earn from investing rather than saving ($400,000 v.s $31,000) is much greater because it grows exponentially, while your savings grow linearly. A person who saves his money will only see an increase in his wealth by the same amount each year. As a saver Billy saw his savings grow by $50 each month. However, while he invested, the amount of money he made each year grew exponentially.

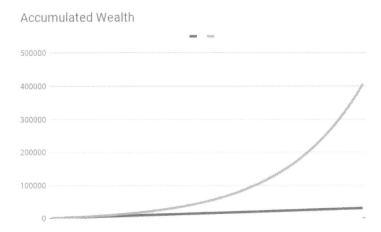

Accumulated Wealth

The graph compares the accumulated wealth if the investor saves and invests his money. It is clear that, with only an average return, the investor clearly makes more money by investing in the stock market because his portfolio grows by a greater amount each year.

Year	Investment	Earnings	Balance
Start	$1,000		$1,000
1	$600.00	$105.70	$1,705.70
2	$600.00	$162.16	$2,467.86
3	$600.00	$223.13	$3,290.99
4	$600.00	$288.98	$4,179.97
5	$600.00	$360.08	$5,140.05
6	$600.00	$436.89	$6,176.94
7	$600.00	$519.85	$7,296.79
8	$600.00	$609.46	$8,506.25
9	$600.00	$706.18	$9,812.43
10	$600.00	$810.70	$11,223.13
11	$600.00	$923.54	$12,746.67
12	$600.00	$1,045.43	$14,392.10
13	$600.00	$1,177.07	$16,169.17
14	$600.00	$1,319.23	$18,088.40
15	$600.00	$1,472.77	$20,161.17
16	$600.00	$1,638.60	$22,399.77
17	$600.00	$1,817.68	$24,817.45
18	$600.00	$2,011.10	$27,428.55
19	$600.00	$2,219.99	$30,248.54
20	$600.00	$2,445.59	$33,294.13
21	$600.00	$2,689.23	$36,583.36
22	$600.00	$2,952.36	$40,135.72
23	$600.00	$3,236.54	$43,972.26
24	$600.00	$3,543.45	$48,115.71
25	$600.00	$3,874.97	$52,590.68
26	$600.00	$4,232.94	$57,423.62
27	$600.00	$4,619.60	$62,643.22
28	$600.00	$5,037.16	$68,280.38
29	$600.00	$5,488.12	$74,368.50
30	$600.00	$5,975.16	$80,943.66
31	$600.00	$6,501.19	$88,044.85
32	$600.00	$7,069.27	$95,714.12
33	$600.00	$7,682.83	$103,996.95
34	$600.00	$8,345.47	$112,942.42
35	$600.00	$9,061.10	$122,603.52
36	$600.00	$9,834.00	$133,037.52
37	$600.00	$10,668.69	$144,306.21
38	$600.00	$11,570.20	$156,476.41
39	$600.00	$12,543.80	$169,620.21
40	$600.00	$13,595.30	$183,815.51
41	$600.00	$14,730.94	$199,146.45
42	$600.00	$15,957.42	$215,703.87
43	$600.00	$17,282.00	$233,585.87
44	$600.00	$18,712.54	$252,898.41
45	$600.00	$20,257.57	$273,755.98
46	$600.00	$21,926.15	$296,282.13

47	$600.00	$23,723.27	$320,610.40
48	$600.00	$25,674.53	$346,884.93
49	$600.00	$27,776.48	$375,261.41
50	$600.00	$30,046.60	$405,908.01

Column one of the table shows which year it is. Column two shows the amount of money Billy invested each year out of pocket; this number is constant. Column three shows the appreciation of his portfolio. It is important to notice that the values in column three grow each year when he invests; the growth grows. During year one, the value of appreciation is $105 while during year two it is $162. Each year, the growth expressed in dollars grows while the growth rate as a percentage remains the same because Billy reinvests the appreciation back into his portfolio. For example, the $105 that Billy made during the first year was reinvested during the second year. Since there were a larger principal and the same growth *rate*, the money grew by a larger value. The earnings from the second year, the $162, was reinvested in the third year, allowing Billy to make $223 that year. However, in order to increase the dollar growth rate, it is crucial that an investor reinvests his profits in order to make more money each year; this is compound interest. When one reinvests his money in order to make more money, the amount of money he makes in the long term grows exponentially. By the end of Billy's 50th year, the growth would have compounded so much to the point where he is making $30,000 per year from investing, assuming an average market return. However, if he did not reinvest his profits and avoided compound interest, he would not be making much money on the 50th year; he would make roughly $2500 per year if he did not reinvest his profits. Thus, by the example of Billy, it is crucial for all new investors to reinvest their profits and to invest rather than save their money because it allows anyone to accumulate the greatest amount of wealth in the long run.

Opening a Brokerage

"Why not invest your assets in the companies you really like? As Mae West said, 'too much of a good thing can be wonderful.'"
-Warren Buffett

In order to invest in stocks, one must set up a brokerage account. A brokerage is a place where you can go to buy and sell stocks. Many brokerages also provide information on every single company that is publicly traded[4]. The brokerage is like the Amazon for stocks. At Amazon, you can learn about many products, and you can buy and sell them. Similarly, a brokerage is a business where you can go and shop for stocks. But, there is a major difference between Amazon and a brokerage firm; Whenever Amazon sells something, they keep a percentage of the profit from the transaction while a brokerage has no rights to any profit made from the transaction. Brokers make their money from charging fees, typically $5, whenever someone buys or sells a stock; to buy a stock and profit from it, you will need to make a $10 gain to break even. The fee is typically flat no matter what the size of the transaction is. On the other hand, Amazon's profit grows with the size of the transaction; if someone sells an expensive product on their website, Amazon's commission will be large compared to

---

[4] A publicly traded company just means that it is a company that you can buy.

if the product was cheap. Thus, in order to buy stocks, you must go to a brokerage, which will charge investors a flat fee of $5 to make a transaction. However, in order to "shop" at a brokerage, you must first have an account with a brokerage.

All brokerages require new investors to have certain information on hand in order to open up an account:

1. Name
2. Social Security Number
3. Date of Birth
4. Phone Number
5. Email address
6. Bank Account Information

The law requires all brokerages to ask this information. Once you have the information needed to open an account, it will be important to decide which "shop" you want to open an account with. There are many options: Fidelity, Robinhood, E-Trade, etcetera. Each of these brokerages has unique perks, and one brokerage is not the best for everyone because each investor has different needs.

However, one brokerage is the best for beginner investors: Robinhood. Robinhood is a broker, like all others, but it has one beneficial characteristic for beginner investors; they do not charge transaction fees. This will allow a beginner investor to save $10 every time he buys and sells his shares, thus increasing his profit. This is especially significant for beginner investors because they typically don't have lots of funds to start investing with. Thus, beginner investors should use Robinhood as their broker because it will increase their profits.

The Strategy

"Only buy something that you'd be perfectly happy to hold if the market shut down for 10 years."
        -Warren Buffett

The first step for any new investor is to figure out his strategy. In recent years, many investing strategies have become prominent: short selling, options trading, swing trading, day trading, etcetera. However, only one strategy best suits a new investor in the stock market. In this chapter, we will look at each of the trading strategies and we will conclude which one is the best for a new investor.

But first, we will consider the characteristics of a good strategy for the beginner investor. A good strategy should first allow any investor with little money to start investing; there should be low barriers to entry. For example, some investing strategies require large sums of money, which most beginner investors do not have. The second characteristic of a beginner-friendly strategy is that it should not be risky for the investor. The strategy should be safe and it should allow an investor to make money in stocks most of the time. Although there is always the possibility of losing money in the stock market, an investor should not put himself in a position to take lots of risk because it can hurt his own financial stability. Many well-known investors, like Warren Buffett, will deem strategies that pose a lot of risk as gambling because those strategies rely more on probability than skill. A trading strategy should also provide an opportunity for the investor to yield a large profit. Many strategies allow investors to gain 1%-2% in capital appreciation in a day. Although these strategies allow an investor to make money in the stock market, the gains are quite small for the time dedication required to invest. Thus, the time a person spends investing would not be worth it unless he has a large amount of capital, which many beginners do not have, to compensate for the small percent gains. Basic criteria for a good investing strategy includes the following: it must provide an adequate return, have low-barriers to entry, and it should not be risky for the investor.

The most popular strategy among new investors is actually one of the worst for them. Day trading is where an investor holds a stock for a couple of hours and then sells it, typically before the market closes, and makes a quick return on an investment. Many new investors see the advertisements of people who claim that they trade for a few hours a day, make thousands of dollars, and all with an easy and teachable strategy. They then try to sell you their course in which you can become just like them. Most of these investors are legit and they do have strategies that will work for some people. However, day trading is not a suitable strategy for a beginner investor. First off, day trading requires an investor to have large sums of capital on hand before he starts to day trade. The Federal Trade Commission requires, by law, for all day traders to maintain a minimum account balance of $25,000 or else their account can be shut down. Considering that most people reading a book on the stock market are looking to build wealth, $25,000 of free cash can be a large sum of money to come up with. Also, most people would fall victim to the transaction fees. When an investor wants to buy a stock, most brokers charge a fee of about $5. The same goes for when he wants to sell, creating a total transaction fee of roughly $10. Given that a day trader usually does not make more than 2% on a good trade, an investor would need to invest $500 daily in order to break even. In order to make a decent gain, he would need to invest several thousand dollars. For most laymen, especially the beginner investor, several thousand dollars in free cash is hard to come up with. Thus, day trading poses many financial challenges for a beginner investor.

Day trading also creates major conflicts with one's lifestyle. Day traders trade from 9:30 am till 4:00 pm, depending on one's time zone. It requires a trader to devote attention to the stock market for many hours without distractions. Most people who aspire to build wealth, work during the day from 8:00 am till 5:00 pm. Day trading would at least require a beginner investor to cut back on his working hours. This will prevent him from getting a full-time job since he would not be able to commit to the hours. He would also have to forgo the benefits of working full time and risk losing a stable source of income. The instability day trading can create for a beginner investor makes it a poor option for the beginner investor.

A beginner investor should also consider the other trading strategies as a possibility: short selling, options, swing trading and long-term investing. The next strategy we will investigate is short selling. Short selling is when an investor *borrows* shares of stock from a person who has invested in the company, and immediately sells the shares. He then hopes that the price of a share goes down in value so he can repurchase the shares at a cheaper price in order to return the shares to the lender. Since he repurchases and returns the shares when they are cheaper, the profit is the difference between the market price when he borrowed and returned the shares at. Although this strategy seems quite easy and safe, especially when you take into account that most of the time new investors lose money when they try to make money, it contains many hidden risks for investors.

      The first of which is that there is no limit on the risk for investors. When an investor purchases shares of stock, he puts all of his money at risk; if the corporation goes bankrupt, he will lose all of his money but, he cannot lose more than the amount he invested. However, with short selling, there is no limit on the loss for a short seller. In 2013, a lot of short sellers borrowed Tesla's stock (TSLA), a company which was struggling to bring in any profits. In fact, they were losing money so, it was a logical idea to short Tesla; many people believed that they would go bankrupt. However, Tesla's stock spiked up over 330% over the next five months. Short sellers had to buy back shares for the lender at a price over 330% of what they borrowed the shares at; since the stock price more than doubled, short sellers lost more money than they actually invested. Notice how a short seller faces the possibility to lose all of their money plus more while a traditional stock market investor can only lose the money he invests. When investors take on the possibility of unlimited risk, it would be safer to not invest in the stock market since investing may hurt one's ability to achieve financial success due to the possibility of owing money. Especially for people who are new to the stock market, short selling is not a safe way to invest in the stock market.

The other way a person can make money on the stock market is through options. Options is, by far, highly confusing to new investors and should not be considered as a choice for the beginner investor. However, we will still look at what options trading is and why investors should avoid it for the completeness of the chapter. Note that I will explain options at the most basic level using layman's vocabulary in order for the reader to understand options.

Investors have two choices when investing in options. They can either purchase a call option or a put option. A call option is a bet that the stock price will go up. When an investor buys a call option, they are buying the right to buy one-hundred shares of stock before a specific date. The price at which an investor buys the call option is called the strike price. So if an investor purchases a call option for 3M (mmm) at a strike price of $100 that expires in two years, the investor has the right to buy 100 shares of 3m within the span of two years. If the price goes up to $110, he makes one-thousand dollars($10 per share*100 shares). But if the market price falls below the value of the strike price and it does not recover, the investor will lose all of his money. If the contract says he has the right to buy shares of 3m at $100 but, if the market price is $85, any investor will be better off to buy the shares at the market price over the contract. On the flip side, if an investor believes the stock price will go down, he can buy a put option.

Although with options trading an investor can bring in large sums of money, the risks and costs outweigh the benefits of options for the beginner investor. First off, no beginner investor will be able to start options trading due to the barriers to entry. All brokerages like Fidelity, Charles Schwab, and E-Trade require an investor to have a large number of assets and experience in the stock market in order to start investing in options. No beginner investor has the capacity to start off in options due to the years of experience that is required in order to trade options. The barriers to entry are there for good reasons though; options trading is a highly risky way to make money in the stock market. No one has the capacity to predict the price of a stock, in the short term, because many factors, which are unknown and not under the investor control, can fluctuate a stock price. For example, many options traders who bought a call option on Amazon (AMZN), a highly stable and successful company that dominates the market place, on August of 2018 lost all of their money due to an unforeseen market correction. Due to a factor that investors have no control over, many options traders lost all of their money. Thus, the risk that options traders take is a large risk for a beginner investor, especially when one considers that the results that an investor gets are largely not under his own control. Rather, it is under the control of luck. Therefore, the beginner investor should avoid options trading.

The next strategy and frankly the least exciting one is called, value investing. Value investing is when an investor looks for companies that are trading below what they are actually worth. If a person believes that a stock should be valued at $80 per share but it is currently trading at $70, the investor would buy the stock while it is cheap because, in the long run, he believes the price will go back up. It is like Black Friday shopping for stocks. Many investors believe that value investing is the optimal strategy for the beginner investor.

First off, value investing allows investors to control the risk that they take. Two types of risks are prominent when investing in stocks. The first is a market price risk. The risk is that an investor will lose money if the share price falls and does not recover. Although an investor does not have direct control over the share price, he is able to mitigate his risks through proper research and stock selection. The second is a business failure risk. It occurs when the shareholder loses all of his money if the corporation fails and goes bankrupt. An investor is also able to avoid the business failure risk through proper research and analysis. Thus, the risk with value investing can be minimized, as long as an investor is not reckless, making it ideal for a beginner investor.

The gains associated with value investing are also substantial. Studies have shown that, on average, a long-term investor can expect an average annual return of 8% per year while many day traders only earn an average annual return of 6% per year, even though they spend more time investing. Compared to other trading strategies, this allows investors to make a large sum of money without having to devote a large amount of time. Since value investing requires less time in managing a portfolio in the long run, it has a much lower opportunity cost. Furthermore, unlike day trading which requires an investor to make drastic changes to his or her lifestyle, a value investor does not need to make those changes because his research can be done during his free time.

The best part about value investing is that anyone can become an investor. A person can open up an account with a brokerage at any time and start to trade stocks as long as he has some money. Thus, value investing fits the third criteria for a good trading strategy for a beginner investor; there are low barriers to entry.

Over the course of the rest of the book, we will take a look at how a beginner investor should value invest in order to become a successful investor.

The Logic Of Value Investing

"Be fearful when others are greedy. Be greedy when others are fearful."
    -Warren Buffett

I am going to ask you a question that any experienced investor can easily answer. Do you buy a stock when the price is going up or going down? Most beginner investors will incorrectly answer this question. Before I answer this question, let me rephrase it in terms of buying t-shirts. Suppose that you went to Walmart yesterday and you saw a shirt that you like. However, you decided not to buy it since it was expensive at the price of $70. The next day, you go back to Walmart and you see the exact same shirt for only $35. The same shirt is 50% off and you believe that it will never be available at such a low price. Do you buy it? In this chapter, we will explore why investors should purchase a stock while the price is going down and not when the price is at its all-time high.

The first hump to get over for beginner investors is to understand why buying a stock while its price is shooting up is bad for investors. But why? Well, take a look at the shirt example. If an item is on sale, it should be seen as a discount, and people should buy it. While the price is high, it should be seen as expensive, and people should wait for a sale. The same principle applies for stocks. If a stock is cheap, it should seem more attractive to investors than if the share price is high because the investor is getting the same exact item- a portion of the company. Would you rather pay more or less for the same thing? Nonetheless, some beginner investors still believe that it is good to invest in a stock when the price is going up because it has momentum or because other people are buying it, so why don't I? This is actually the strategy that many day traders use. They wait for upward momentum and usually buy and sell their shares in minutes. However, for a value investor, an investor the goes for a big gain in the long run, such a strategy will only introduce him to big losses. The best way to demonstrate the weakness in a momentum-trading strategy is through case studies. In August 2018, Apple (AAPL) hit a trillion dollar market cap. Many investors thought that this meant that they should invest in the stock because its price was trending upwards. So many people did invest in Apple, causing the share price to climb quickly. It increased by over 15% within one month. However, by the end of a few months, the stock price came crashing down as fast as it went up; It fell by about $50 or 25%. Although some investors cashed out before it crashed, many investors were unable to and got caught in the fall. The main problem with trading on the uptrend is that there is no signal on when to sell a stock. Investors do not know when the share price will fall back down. Also, when investors look to ride the momentum, they typically experience small gains compared to that of the value investor because they are using a day trader's strategy, which only aims for small gains in a short period of time; momentum trading will only yield small profits because the strategy is not made to yield large, long-term gains. Rather, it is made for smaller, short-term profits. Thus, it is optimal to buy a stock when it is cheap in order to maximize an investor's long-term profits.

Beginner investors must be able to identify when a stock is undervalued. Looking at a share price does not necessarily tell the whole story. Since, for every company, there are a different amount of shares in the market, every firms' share price will be different even if they have the same valuation. Thus, investors should not look at the share price to determine if a company is cheap. Rather, they should look at the PE ratio. The PE ratio is the price to earnings ratio. It is calculated by dividing the price per share by the earnings per share. It measures the priceyness of a stock relative to profit. If there are two companies, one with a PE ratio of 15 and one with a PE ratio of 25, the firm with the PE ratio of 15 would be considered cheaper, even if it has a higher stock price, because it is cheaper to "own" $1 of earnings in the company with a PE ratio of 15; it only costs $15 to "own" one dollar of earnings in company with a PE ratio of 15 while it costs $25 to "own" $1 of earnings in a company with a PE ratio of 25 (The word "own" is in quotation marks because an investor technically does not own the earnings of a company, as explained in the chapter called "What is a Stock"). An investor needs to be careful when he uses the PE ratio to compare corporations because PE ratios can only compare companies that are in the same industry. An investor cannot compare the PE ratio of a tech company with a healthcare company to see if one is cheaper. The investor must compare firms in the same industry. For example, he can compare the PE ratios of two health care companies.

However, investors must be aware of the value trap. It occurs when an investor buys a stock just because its stock price is going down. This can be detrimental to a beginner investor's portfolio. For example, if an investor purchased shares in Snapchat (SNAP) when the price was going down, the investor would be down in the long run because the company has been seeing a declining number of users; less users means less profitability, and less profitability means stock price will be declining. Some new investors saw this as a good buy since the price was low and they decided to buy the stock. They lost lots of money. Snapchat's stock teaches an important lesson to new investors: always look at why the stock price is going down. Snapchat's stock was declining because the actual company was declining. It is not a good idea to invest in a company if the company is starting to decline. Rather, a beginner investor wants to invest in companies that are still growing when they have a low or declining stock price. In many instances, although it is contradictory, the stock price is declining while the company is still growing and prosperous. That is when a beginner investor should buy shares in a company. For example, at the end of December 2018, stocks were falling because many believed a stock market crash was coming and that the trade war was going to get worse. This caused many stock prices to fall, even though many of the companies were still growing. One of these companies was Amazon (AMZN). In December Amazon fell over 20% due to the reasons mentioned above, even though the company was experiencing large increases in revenue growth every year. Notice how the stock price drastically fell even though the company was even better! If investors bought it at the lows, they would be up over 20% in less than 30 days. It is important to understand the difference between Amazon's case and Snapchat's case. In Snapchat's case, the stock price fell because the company was declining. In Amazon's case, the stock price fell not because the company was declining, rather, it fell for reasons unrelated to the business valuation; Amazon's business was cheaper even though it was rapidly growing. When a product gets cheaper, it is a better buy as long as it is the same or better quality. If the shirt price was lowered because it was torn apart, like Snapchat, then one should not buy it because it was lower in quality. However, if the shirt's quality was improving and the price was getting cheaper, like Amazon, almost anyone would buy the shirt. It is the same thing with stocks. Beginner investors should invest in quality businesses that are improving in spite of their falling valuation.

Cash Is King: When To Buy A Stock

"Never take your eyes off the cash flow because it's the lifeblood of business."
- Sir Richard Branson

The most crucial and difficult part about investing in stocks is determining the right time to buy. The main reason all beginner investors have trouble with determining the right price is due to a poor understanding of why a company is valuable at certain valuations, and not at other valuations.

In order to understand why certain valuations are attractive, a beginner investor should imagine himself purchasing the entire company by paying the value of the market capitalization[5]. Then he needs to determine if the firm makes enough profit for the beginner investor, within a reasonable amount of time, if he purchases the entire company at the value of the market capitalization. If the beginner investor believes that he would be profitable if he purchased the entire company, then it is potentially a good investment. For example, if a firm averages $10,000 in net-income every year, but it is currently trading at a valuation of $500,000, it is very unlikely that he will make his money

---

[5] The market capitalization or valuation of a company is equal to the number of shares outstanding times the share price. It represents the amount of money an investor would need to buy every single share of the company.

back anytime soon; it will take 50 years to break even, making it an undesirable investment. However, if the firm was making $10,000 per year, but only trading at a valuation of $40,000, the investor would be able to break even by the 4th year, if he purchases the entire company, allowing him to make long-run profits. The second firm is potentially a good investment because it is trading at a fair valuation; it would allow the investor to make profits in the long run, if he purchases the entire company. It is important to note that when an investor purchases a company on the stock exchange, he does not receive the actual profits of the company, but he sees the value of his equity and shares rise. The value of equity rising when owning stock is similar to being profitable when owning a company. Nonetheless, the beginner investor should run this type of analysis for every single company and he should invest in the companies that he believes will be the most profitable for him if he purchases it at the value of the market capitalization.

   If an investor knows a firm's future profits, he would be able to determine an attractive price to pay for a company. For example, if a beginner investor wants to buy shares in a lemonade stand, and if he knows that in 5 years the stand will have a total profit of $1000, the investor knows that its valuation (market capitalization) must be $1000 or less in order to be profitable by the 5th year. However, he cannot see into the future, and he does not know the future profits of the firm. If he knew this for every company, he would instantly know if an investment would be profitable because he would know the current cost to purchase the company (current market capitalization) and the amount of money it will make him (future net income) in the future. Thus, if an investor knew a firm's future profits, he would instantly be successful.

However, since we do not have such information, it is the main job of the investor to predict the firm's future profits. The best way investors can do this is by following Phil Town's method, which he outlines in his book called *Rule #1*. He outlays the steps, which will be covered in this chapter, to predict a company's future value by predicting its future earnings. First, we will cover how to find the numbers you need for the calculation.

The first metric we will need is the current earnings per share (EPS). The EPS can be found on Yahoo Finance, under the summary tab. It is located under the PE ratio. This metric represents the net income for each share of stock that exists, and it represents how much profit "belongs" to you for each share of stock you own.

The next metric we need is the equity growth rate. Equity is equal to a firm's assets minus its liabilities. It represents the assets that are left for the owners after all the debt is paid off. The equity growth rate shows by how much the value of the shareholders' assets, which tends to be a surplus of cash, grows each year. There are two ways to obtain this valuable metric. The first is by using the rule of 72 to predict the average annual growth rate. The rule of 72 states that if a person divides 72 by the annual growth rate, he will have the time (in years) it will take for the principal to double. For example, if I invested $100,000 into the S&P 500, and assuming it grows at an average rate of 10% per year, we can calculate the amount of time it will take for my investment to double by dividing 72 by the annual growth rate of 10%: 72/10. 7.2 years is the amount of time for my investment to double to $200,000, which we calculated by dividing 72 by the annual growth rate of 10%. It is important to not enter the annual growth rate as a percent (.1) because the math will not work. Rather, he should enter it as a whole number. If an investment grows at an average rate of 10% per year, he should enter the number 10 instead of .1 or 10%. The rule of 72 also says that if a person divides 72 by the number of years it take something to double, he will get the annual growth rate. For example, if I know it will take 7.2 years for my investment of $100,000 to double to $200,000, we can divide 72 by the time it will take the investment to double, 7.2 years, to get the annual growth rate of 10% per year: 72/7.2=10. Thus, to get the annual growth rate, an investor can divide 72 by the time it takes for an investment to double. Now that we understand the rule of 72, we can use it to predict the annual equity growth rate of a company. We will walk through a sample calculation using Twitter's (TWTR) financial data and the rule of 72. To do this we can go on a stock's balance sheet and find the metric labeled "equity", which is near the bottom of a balance sheet. As a reminder, the balance sheet can be found on Yahoo Finance and under the financials tab. We need to find the time it takes for the equity to double in order to calculate the annual growth rate of equity. According to Twitter's balance sheet, total equity was roughly $3.6 billion in 2014, and it (roughly) doubled to $6.8 billion by 2018. (For the purposes of the calculations, we need to find the time for the equity to *roughly* double. From 2014 to 2018, Twitter's equity increased by a factor of 1.89, which means that it almost doubled. Since it almost doubled, an investor should round 1.89 to 2 and assume that it doubled during those four years because a company's equity will never exactly double. In short, it is safe to round your numbers and assume that equity doubled when it *nearly* doubled). If we divided 72 by 4, the number of years it took for equity to roughly double, we will find that Twitter has an annual equity growth rate of 18%. This number will be important for calculating the stock's future value.

The second way to find the annual equity growth rate is by going on Zacks.com. Zacks is a website, similar to Yahoo Finance, where an investor can find information about a company. After an investor gets a quote for a stock he is researching, he should scroll down to where it says "Exp (expected) EPS Growth Rate" under the "Key Earnings Data" tab.

This value should be roughly the same as the one calculated with the rule of 72. For Twitter, this value is 23.5%. However, there should be some difference between the two values because the equity growth rate we calculated with the rule of 72 was a measurement of a past growth rate and the metric on Zacks is a measurement of a predicted, future growth rate. However, we can assume that the past growth rate will be relatively similar to the future growth rate because we are investing in companies that have strong moats. Meaning, their profitability is not volatile because it is difficult to compete with the firms we invest in. Hence, their profitability is predictable and stable, allowing us to assume that the past growth rate will be similar to the future growth rate. Nonetheless, once we have the two growth rates from Zacks and the rule of 72, we need to decide which one we will use in the final calculation. The general rule with business is to stay conservative with your numbers, meaning to use the metric that is the least optimistic because it will account for unforeseen matters like an unexpected drop in sales or a large litigation expense; for growth rates, the more conservative number is the smaller one. Thus, we will use 18% instead of 23.5% as our equity growth rate for our final calculation because it is more conservative.

The next metric we need to figure out is the future PE ratio. As a reminder, the PE ratio is the price per share divided by the earnings per share. It represents the cost to "attain" one dollar of a company's annual earnings. A low PE ratio tends to be associated with slow-growing and cheaper companies while a high PE ratio is associated with fast-growing and expensive stocks. Nonetheless, in order to find the future PE ratio of a company, we can take the average of its historical PE ratios because they tend to be the same for a company over the span of 10 years. Since the companies we invest in are large, dominant, and well-protected with moats, these firms are unlikely to experience robust growth nor a dramatic decline; the growth and investor sentiment of these companies are not volatile, allowing them to maintain a relatively stable PE ratio over time. It is important to take the historical PE ratio of the stock over the past 10 years because, over a span of 5 years, cyclical[6] developments could have affected this value, and

---

[6] In business, the word "cyclical" refers to the business cycle in which the economy goes through periods of expansions and recessions. Typically, a stock's data fluctuates in the short term if there is a recession or expansion. So, it is best to look at data over a longer period of time, because less of the data will be affected by a volatile economy.

if an investor takes the value over a span of 20 years, many fundamentals and prospects about this business could have changed. So, 10 years is a good balance. In order to find the metric, we have to use a less conventional website because many financial sites like Yahoo Finance and Zacks do not track this information. If an investor goes to macrotrends.net, types in the stock ticker symbol, and clicks on the "PE ratio" tab, he will find three charts. For the purposes of the calculation, the third chart is the most important. The third chart contains data of a company's PE ratio history. We want to make an educated, rough estimate of the PE ratio of the last 10 years. This is the number we will use as the predicted PE ratio in our calculation. By looking at the graph below, we can estimate that the PE ratio is roughly 15 over the past years. Thus, in order to obtain the future PE ratio, which is similar to the historical PE ratio, an investor can go to macrotrends.net and take the average of the PE ratios over the last 10 years.

Historical PE Ratios found on macrotrends.net

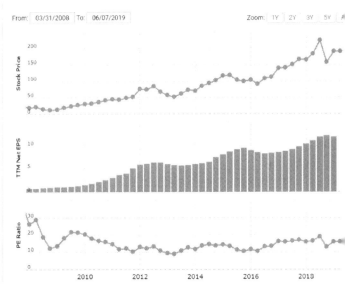

The last metric that we need to know in order to calculate an attractive price to buy a stock at, is the desired rate of return. This is the percent gain an investor wants to achieve. Since beginner investors are putting in the effort to buy good businesses, they should aim to beat the S&P 500. Hence, the desired rate of return should be greater than 10%. 15% is a reasonable goal to strive for. Thus, the desired rate of return is 15%.

Here is a summary of how to get the metrics to predict the future value of a stock:

1. EPS: Can be found on the summary tab of any financial website.
2. Future Equity Growth Rate (Expected EPS Growth Rate): Can be calculated by dividing 72 by the number of years it takes the historical equity of a

firm to double. We can use historical growth rates to predict future growth rates because we are investing in firms with strong moats that are stable. This number can also be obtained from the stock overview page on Zacks.com. We will use the lower value of the two in order to stay conservative.

3. Future PE ratio: Can be found by taking the average of the firm's PE ratios over the last 10 years. The historical PE ratios can be found on macrotrends.net, under the PE ratios tab, and on the third chart. We can use the historical PE ratios to predict future PE ratios because they tend to stay relatively the same over time, for established firms.

4. Desired return on investment: 15% is the fixed, desired rate of return because investors should aim to beat the market.

Now, we have to use these numbers to calculate the price we should pay for a stock. Let's assume that for the following calculation, the stock has a current EPS of $2 per share, an annual growth rate of 24% and a future PE ratio of 12.

The first step is to use the rule of 72 to figure out the number of years it will take for the EPS to double at its current growth rate. To calculate this, an investor can divide 72 by 24 to get 3; it will take 3 years for EPS to double.

The next step is to use the answer calculated in the previous step to estimate the firm's earnings per share in 10 years. Since we know that it takes three years for its EPS to double, we know it will double roughly three times (10 years/3 years to double= 3.33 doubles). So it will go from $2 to $4 per share after 3 years, from $4 to $8 per share after 3 more years, and from $8 to $16 per share by the 9th year. Thus, we can calculate the EPS of a stock 10 years into the future by calculating the number of times it will double in 10 years. As a side note, it is ideal to use 10 years as the timeframe because 5 years is too short to predict the stock price because cyclical developments can affect the price, and 20 years tends to be too far into the future to accurately predict the stock price. So, 10 years tends to be ideal.

Nonetheless, once an investor has the expected future earnings per share, he needs to use it to calculate the future price of the stock. To do this, the beginner investor has to multiply the expected PE ratio and the expected EPS in 10 years. Multiplying these two values will yield the predicted market price of the stock in 10 years. Using the numbers above, we would multiply 12, the expected PE ratio, and 16, the expected EPS, to get a future market price of $192.

The second to last step is to calculate the present-day intrinsic value of the stock. This metric represents a fair price to purchase the stock in order to achieve a desired return of 15% per year. In order to calculate it, a beginner investor should divide 72 by 15, the minimum acceptable rate of return, to find the time it takes for his investment to double; it's roughly 5 years. That means, in 10 years, his investment will double 2 times. If we know that it is ideal for a beginner investor's investment to double 2 times over the span of 10 years, then we know that a fair market price is ¼ of the future market price because the fair, present-day market price*2*2=future market price; we multiply by 2 twice because the investment will double 2 times from the fair market price with a 15% return in order to get to the future market price. Since we already found the future market price of the stock by multiplying its expected EPS and PE ratio, we can plug $192, the future market price, into the equation and divide it by 4 (2*2). This will give us a fair, present-day market price of $48. Since a beginner investor should always aim to make 15% per year, the equation, fair price*2*2=future market price, will always be true because the 2*2 portion is derived from aiming for a return of 15% per year. In short, we are able to divide the stock's future market price by 4 in order to find a fair price to purchase the stock at.

If an investor purchases the stock at the fair value, ¼ of the future value, he will likely come close to achieving an average return of 15% per year. However, due to rounding in the calculations, cyclical developments in the market, and unpredictable stock price fluctuations, it is important to buy the stock with a margin of safety- a protection against error. The margin of safety price can be calculated by taking 20% of the fair price. The margin of safety price is like the Black-Friday, sale price of a stock, while the fair stock price, which is ¼ of the future value, is like the regular, retail price of a stock. In order to maximize gains, account for calculation errors, and mitigate risk, beginner investors want to purchase the stock at the sale price. Beginner investors want to purchase the stock with at least a 20% discount of the retail or fair price because it will allow him to mitigate risk of accidentally buying too high or overlooking weak business characteristics. If the fair price is $48, a beginner investor wants to purchase the stock at $38.40 ($48*.8) or less. This will also allow the investor to also make a larger profit. Thus, an investor should wait till the market price falls at least 20% below the present-day, fair price to purchase the stock at its Black Friday price.

10-K

"Never invest in a business you cannot understand."
-Warren Buffett

The 10-K is a firm's annual report. It has everything an investor needs to know about a business. The annual report is released every year by the company itself. They recap successes and failures of the year, and they set goals and objectives for the next year. The firm also presents its financial data in the 10-K. Much of this information is presented on Yahoo Finance but, there are some key elements which are not presented on Yahoo Finance. This chapter will highlight key sections of the annual report.

The first step is to find the annual report. If a beginner investor googles a company he wants to research followed by the words annual report, the first website that will appear is the company's investor relations page. For example, if an investor wants to read Kellogg's (K) annual report, he or she should google "Kellogg 10-k" to find their investor relations page. Then, if a beginner investor clicks on the investor relations page, a link to a pdf of the annual report will appear on that page.

The first thing the investor should look at is the section called "Business". It is important for investors to read this page because it tells the investor about the business model. It gives a summary of the business and how it operates. It usually teaches something new. It is important to read this section because investors should never invest in something without fully understanding it because it will prevent him from making intelligent decisions. For example, if an investor is unable to understand the marketplace, he may not foresee new competition that could take much of the firm's market share. Also, if an investor does not understand how the firm operates, he will not feel confident holding the stock when its price falls; if someone does not understand what they are buying, they should not buy it. Thus, the business section of the annual report will allow the investor to understand the business, which is crucial for long-term investing.

The next important section to read is the section called "risk factors." It shares factors the firm believes can hinder their performance in upcoming years. It is straightforward yet important for investors to read because it can reveal hindsight on the investor's end. When an investor reads it, he has to make sure he is comfortable with the risks involved. If the investor does not feel comfortable with the risks, he should not invest in the business because, if one of the risks impacts the business, it can cause emotional stress in the long run. Thus, the investor should read about the business model and risk factors in the annual report in order to avoid unnecessary risk.

Emotional Intelligence

"The trick is not to learn to trust your gut feelings, but rather to discipline yourself to ignore them. Stand by your stocks as long as the fundamental story of the company hasn't changed."
-Peter Lynch

It does not matter whether someone is a hard worker, or if he is an excellent stock picker, he will lose in the stock market if he does not have emotional intelligence. Almost all beginner investors do not have much emotional intelligence until they learn the importance of it. This chapter will take a look at what emotional intelligence is and why it is crucial for new investors to have it.

Although I said that we would look at what emotional intelligence is, unlike other investing terms, there is no exact definition for it. It is like trying to define the word intelligent. Is someone intelligent if he has good grades? Does that exclude high school dropouts like Bill Gates from being intelligent? Are people intelligent if they are rich? What if they were born rich? The point is there is no exact nor correct definition of intelligence and, the same goes for emotional intelligence. Rather, the best way to define emotional intelligence is by looking at the characteristics of an emotionally intelligent person.

The first characteristic of an emotionally intelligent person is that he makes rational buying decisions. Many new investors will purchase a stock, even though it goes against the fundamental analysis that this book advocates for. This can occur in multiple forms and, we will cover some of the most common ways this manifests itself so that you can avoid making big mistakes.

The first way beginner investors will irrationally buy stocks is by buying a stock when they see the price going up; they feel that the price will go higher and higher, so they buy and try to time the market and sell the shares when the price is even higher, so that they can make a quick buck. For multiple reasons, this is one of the most common and most dangerous decisions a new investor can make in the stock market. First off, when he starts to trade off stock price for short-run gains, he unintentionally starts to gamble without knowing it. The reason it is considered gambling is because he has no evidence or reason to believe that the stock price will go up in the future. Past stock prices do not affect future stock prices, even though the beginner investor might think that the stock price will continue going up because it did in the past. Trading on the basis of stock price does not work for multiple reasons. Many of these reasons were explored in further depth in the chapter called *The Strategy* however, I will touch on some of the main reasons why trading on stock price does not work. The biggest reason is that no one has the power to predict how a stock price will move in the near future. The price is not reflective of anything except the supply and demand for the stock; if there are more buyers (demand) for a stock, the price will increase, and if there are more sellers (supply), the price will decrease. For example, a stock price changes hundreds of times within a couple of hours because the supply and demand changes whenever someone executes a trade. If you see the stock price going up, there are more buyers than sellers for that stock however, it does not mean that the stock price will continue to go up because some people could decide to sell their shares, and the price would go back down. If you bought the stock because the price was going up for a short term trade, your profit would be pure luck because you do not control the short term stock price; you do not control whether other people are buying and selling the stock. Nonetheless, there are many more examples in which emotions overtake the rational mind of beginner investors. This can also happen when an investor wants to sell a stock.

Just like how a beginner investor wants to buy a stock if he sees the price going up, he sometimes wants to sell the stock once the price has gone up a couple percent because he fears that the price will go down; he wants to claim his gains. However, this can be very dangerous. If he sees the price going up and sells too quickly, assuming he did his research and invested in a good company, the stock will grow by much more in the long term. For example, if you purchased Pepsi (Pep) and then saw the price go up by 5%, you might be tempted to sell and take your gains. However, if you wait, over the long term, you can make 10%, 15%, or even 100%. Since 2002, Pepsi's stock has grown by 175%, and the investors are still invested because they know that Pepsi is still a fundamentally good business.

If they sold out early on, they would have lost big gains in the long run. Thus, a beginner investor should always stay in a stock for the long run because it will allow him to see the biggest gains; he must avoid selling early for quick profits.

There are still more situations in which the emotions of an investor can overtake him. This one is probably one of the most dangerous ones; he sells his stock if it goes down. Many new investors, once they buy their stock, sell it if the price of it goes below their initial investment. This is very irrational for multiple reasons, but the biggest reason is that the investor is taking an unnecessary loss; if any investor sells his shares too quickly when it goes down 1%, 3%, or even 10%, he is losing money by his own choice. Many new investors do this because when they see their investments lose money, they want to minimize any losses by selling their shares. However, when someone sells their shares when it goes down, they are actually maximizing their losses because, in the long run, the stock will most likely go up given that you invested in a good company at a good price. Also, no matter what happens, your stock price will go down some days, and other days it will go up because the supply and demand change every day. In fact, it is impossible to buy a stock at the lowest point, according to the best investors like Peter Lynch and Warren Buffett. Since a person cannot predict the lowest price of a stock, it is nearly guaranteed that he will be in the red for some time; this is normal and it is not an investor's fault if he is down in the short term because it is just luck. The best investors do not worry if they are in the red in the short term, while the amateur investors worry about short term price fluctuations. However, if he holds on to a good company and buys at a cheap price, he will most definitely be in the green over the long run. The overall lesson here is to be rational about your buying and selling decisions; if you believe in a company for the long term, hold their stock for the long term, and do not buy or sell it because of short term price fluctuations. When a beginner investor is rational, he will be profitable. If a long term investor does not have such discipline, he will fail at investing. If he wants to build this discipline, which almost all new investors need to do, it is important to avoid checking the price of your stock often. Personally, for new investors, I do not recommend ever checking the stock price during trading hours. This can make an investor feel paranoid about how the price will change during the day. This will also result in the investor checking the stock price more often, making him more paranoid. At most, one should not check on his portfolio more than once per day. It is better to check after trading hours because then, the stock prices are less volatile[7]. It also gives an investor time to make rational decisions because, if he wants to buy or sell a stock, you would have to wait till the next trading day to execute a trade. Thus, in order to build up discipline and avoid making emotional

---

[7] The word volatile just means that the stock price changes a lot. A stock that is not volatile has a stock price that is generally flat.

decisions, it is important that a beginner investor avoids checking the stock price often.

The Most Important Characteristic: A Moat

When we see a moat that's tenuous in any way — it's just too risky.
-Warren Buffett

One of the key features of a successful business is that it has a "moat". A moat is a unique advantage a firm has that prevents competitors from overtaking it; it protects the firm and allows it to be dominant. A moat prevents competitors from taking away a firm's profits and decreasing its stock price. A moat can come in multiple forms, but there are a few common forms that we will discuss. It is crucial that a beginner investor can identify that a firm has a moat because he always wants his firms to have a moat.

The first type of moat is a brand. A brand is a unique feeling a consumer has when he or she uses a product from a certain company. Typically, a brand is an identity of a company that makes it more valuable, and we tend to associate a phrase, symbol, or product with that brand. For example, most people associate the phrase "just do it" with Nike (NKE) or I'm lovin it" with McDonalds (MCD). It is crucial and advantageous if your firm's stock has a brand associated with it because it gives them a loyal customer base, and it prevents competitors from siphoning its profits. For example, Apple (AAPL) is a popular brand among people these days; most people can associate the

Apple logo with the firm, and people are willing to buy a phone from Apple because it's made by Apple. Few people are willing to switch from Apple to Samsung because Apple has a strong brand, even though the phones are quite similar. This guarantees Apple to have consumers when it releases a new phone. This also prevents new telecommunications firms from increasing their market share; consumers are not willing to leave Apple because they are attached to the firm's brand. Apple's brand allows them to grow its consumer base, profits and market share, allowing its stock to grow in value. If a beginner investor invested in a firm like Samsung, that has a weaker brand, it is possible that he will face severe losses because his firm will have trouble maintaining its market share. Thus, a strong brand can provide a beginner investor's stock security.

The next type of moat is a trade secret. A trade secret is a form of intellectual property that allows firms to protect the *recipe* to produce a product. Trade secrets are common in the food and beverage industry. Many firms have a secret recipe that allows them to make a product without others knowing the recipe. One of the most famous trade secrets is the Coca-Cola recipe. The trade secret is so valuable that the recipe is kept in a large, underground vault. For over 100 years, the recipe to make Coca-Cola has been hidden from the public, and it will continue to be a secret, because it prevents other firms from making a similar product and competing with the firm. By preventing other firms from knowing the recipe to make Coca-Cola,

Coke (KO) is able to maintain a monopoly over the product. That means anyone who wants Coca-Cola must buy it from Coke. Firms are unable to compete with Coke because they do not have Coca-Cola. This allows Coke to maintain market share, make a profit, and evade competition, making it less likely that its stock price will fall. Thus, a trade secret, another type of moat, can defend a firm against competition.

The next type of moat is the network-externality moat. A network externality moat is when a good's or service's value rises when there are more people who use it, preventing new competitors who, have no users at the start, from gaining users for providing similar services. Facebook (FB) is a prime example of a firm that has a network-externality moat. Since many people use Facebook, many more people join the platform over other social media platforms just because it is popular. When a firm has a strong, network-externality moat, which occurs when a firm has many users, competitors are unlikely to pose a large threat because it would be hard for a startup competitor to gain users; few users would be willing to join a new platform because people would rather use Facebook because their friends and other users are already on the platform. This allows Facebook to maintain an oligopoly over the social media industry as competing firms cannot find users because of Facebook's network-externality moat.

Investors should always look out for at least one type of moat in the business he invests in because it will protect the firm's profits. When a firm has a moat, it has pricing power- the ability to charge higher prices for the same product- because there are few, threatening competitors. For example, in recent years, consumers have seen Apple raise the price of its iPhone from $499 with the iPhone 6s to over $1000 with the iPhone X. Although the products are similar, Apple is able to charge a high price for the phone because they know that consumers will not buy a phone from another company due to its brand. This allows Apple to make more profit, which allows the firm to expand and grow, raising its stock price.

Moats also make it less likely that the firm will fall in the long-run due to competition. When a firm has a moat, it is much harder for a new, innovative firm to enter the industry and outplay the dominant firm. It is quite common to see industries and companies that have been around for a long time to die or decline because they did not have a moat. For example, 10 years ago, everyone thought the taxi industry would still be around because they are a necessity for many people. However, there were nearly no moats, and anyone could enter the industry if he or she wanted to. Then, by 2018 and 2019, many people use Uber (UBER) drivers instead of conventional taxis because they are more convenient. Uber was able to change the entire taxi industry because there were no moats. Had there been a law that prevented people from driving others unless they were in a taxi, or if a taxi firm had a strong brand, Uber would have not been able to effectively compete in the taxi industry. Thus, taxis would still be the first choice when looking for a chauffeur if there were moats in the taxi industry. If a beginner investor's stock does not have a moat, a new, innovative competitor could enter the industry and destroy a beginner investor's company. Thus, a beginner investor should always invest in firms that have a strong moat because it allows them to maintain control over the industry, and it gives them pricing power.

Financial Characteristics of a Good Stock And Yahoo Finance

"This is one of the keys to successful investing: focus on the companies, not on the stocks."
-Peter Lynch

YahooFinance.com will be one of your most important websites from which you get information about a stock. It is free, and it has almost everything you need to know about a company. This chapter will walk you through how you can maximize the usage of the information the website provides when purchasing stocks.

Once you go to YahooFinance.com, their homepage will come up. On the search bar at the top of the homepage, you can type a company's name in order to start getting information about the company. This will bring you to the summary page of the company. If you feel overwhelmed by all the numbers that pop up, don't worry; you are not alone. For the purposes of long term investing, you only need to know some of this information. The first piece of information is the stock price. The graph on the right shows a history of stock prices. The number that is in red shows the current stock price. Right above the chart, there are characters that read as 1D, 5D, 1m, 6, YTD, 1Y, 5Y, Max. These buttons are used to change the time frame of the chart. The D stands for days, the M stands for months, and the Y stands for years. The YTD stands for year to date and, it will give you the stock price since January first. Max will allow you to see the stock price since its inception. By altering these settings, you can see whether you are purchasing a stock at a relatively expensive or cheap price. Also on the summary page, there is a statistic called PE ratio. This metric was explained in depth in the chapter called *The Logic of Value Investing,* but I will explain it again because it is a good refresher. When you are value investing, you want to look for stocks that have a low PE ratio relative to the industry and the market. The PE ratio stands for price to earnings ratio; it is the price per share divided by the earnings per share. The number represents, in a way, how much money do you have to pay to "own" one dollar of the company's earnings. When a company has a high PE ratio like 100, it means that you have to pay one hundred dollars to "own" one dollar of that company's earnings. On the other hand, if a stock's PE ratio is 12, you have to pay $12 to "own" one dollar of the company's earnings. When a PE ratio is high, it tends to indicate that the company is overvalued while a low PE ratio tends to indicate that the company is undervalued. For the purposes of value investing, we want to look for PE ratios that are low because we want to buy companies when they are cheap and sell them when they are expensive. When a PE ratio is above 30, most value investors would avoid such company because, usually, the investor cannot imagine himself making his money back, if he were to purchase the entire company; oftentimes, investing in firms with high PE ratios can be speculative because there is little cash flow to justify its valuation, as it will be explained in the chapter called *Speculative Stocks*. Since firms with a high PE ratio tend to be expensive for relatively small profits, as a beginner investor, it is best to avoid firms with a high PE ratio; it is better to buy low and sell high rather than buy high and hope to sell higher.

The next important metric to look at is the dividend yield[8]. There are two values in this column: one is in parenthesis and the other number, on the left, is outside the parenthesis. The number on the left shows the annual dollar value of the dividend. This is how much money you will get paid each year for every share of stock you own when the company chooses to pay a dividend. The percentage in the parenthesis- the dividend yield- is the dollar-dividend value divided by the stock price times one hundred. The percentage represents the return on investment from a dividend. For example, if a stock has a 3% dividend yield, the investor will automatically have a 3% gain due to the dividend. This metric is explained more thoroughly in the chapter called *Dividends,* but, in this chapter, we will look

---

[8] For a more in depth discussion about dividends, read the chapter called "Dividends" to learn about how it relates to finding a good stock.

at the importance of a dividend when looking for a stock. Typically, you want most of your stocks to pay dividends as a beginner because it can help mitigate losses when you are first learning about the markets. A dividend also signals that the company is generally stable so, for beginner investors, it is a measure of security. When looking for a dividend paying stock, you typically want to find a stock that pays around a 2%-5% yield. As long as a company is still growing and not plateauing, it is fine if its stock has a yield lower than 2%. However, you also do not want the yield to be over 5% because a high dividend yield might be the result of a falling stock price over the last few years and not of a financially sound firm that can afford to increase its dividend. Also, when a dividend yield gets too high, a divided cut usually follows. Nonetheless, if you choose to invest in a company that pays a higher dividend, it is important to see if the company's financials are sound, as explained in the chapter called *Dividends*.

The next important tab is the tab called "Statistics." Under this tab, most of the statistics are not useful for beginner investors who are looking for a good stock. However, there are some really important statistics under this tab. The first one is the payout ratio. It is all the way on the bottom of the statistics tab, and it is under the heading called *Dividends & Splits*. The payout ratio is the total amount of money firm pays out in dividends divided by the net income times one hundred. It shows the percent of profits that are being paid out as dividends. If this metric is a high value, it means that a large portion of the company's profits are being paid out as dividends. A low number means that a small portion of the company's profits go towards dividends. If a beginner investor wants to hold a dividend-paying stock for a long time, the ideal payout ratio is less than 70%. Companies that have a payout ratio above 70% tend to have too much of their profits being paid out in dividends; if their profits fall by 25%, they will not be able to fully pay their dividends. Moreover, companies with high dividend payout ratios may be susceptible to cutting their dividend because the firm might want to reinvest its profits back into the company. Thus, investors need to look for an ideal payout ratio under the statistics tab in Yahoo Finance.

The next tab- "Historical Data"- is also important for beginner investors. We will use this tab to check the dividend history. First, it is important to change the "Time Period" to "Max", and the "Show" to "Dividend only". Then click apply. This will show investors every time the company paid a dividend. Under this tab, investors should look for positive trends in the dividend payment. If investors want to invest in a company that pays a healthy dividend, it is important to see that the dividend is steadily increasing over many years. It shows that the company is looking to increase its dividends in the future, thus increasing investors' returns. It is also a signal that the management believes that the firm will continue to grow in the future. Investors also need to look for any drops in the dividends. Recent dividend cuts can signal that the company is financially unstable and that the dividend might be cut during the time a new investor owns the stock. It can also signal that the firm is predicting that sales will plateau or fall. Thus, any decrease in the dividend payment should be a warning sign for a beginner investor. A beginner investor should also look for how long the company has been paying the dividend for. If the firm has been paying it for many years, it is likely to be stable. It also shows that the firm is likely to continue to pay a dividend because it helps the stock's track record to keep a dividend-payment streak. In fact, Coca-Cola (KO) has been paying their dividend for almost 100 years, and the management will try to keep the streak because it would make them look bad if they do not; a long history of paying dividend signals that a firm will continue to pay dividends in the future.

On the other hand, if the company just started to pay a dividend, a beginner investor must look into the company's financials and payout ratio to determine if the dividend is stable. Overall, investors need to look for an increasing dividend payment over the firm's dividend-paying history.

One of the most important tabs in Yahoo Finance is called "Financials." It has information on the company's three financial statements: income statement, balance sheet, and cash flow statement. Each of these documents has important information for investors. The first one listed on Yahoo Finance, the income statement, shows the company's income versus their expenses: how much money comes into the business, and how much goes out. On the income statement, it is important to look at the "net income applicable to common shares" and "total revenue." "Net income applicable to common shares" is a synonym for profit. Total revenue is the amount of money that the company brings in, excluding any expenses. It is obvious, yet crucial, that investors look for the revenue and net income to be increasing over the years. Many investors neglect to look at these metrics even though they are key to understanding whether a business is still growing. If investors see these numbers decreasing, it is a bad sign; if this has been occurring over the past couple of years, it is likely that the business is dying. However, even if the business is profitable, it is important to still look at other factors in order to make sure the firm is financially sound.

One can ensure that the firm is financially stable by looking at its balance sheet. The balance sheet is right next to the income statement tab on Yahoo Finance. A balance sheet shows what the company owns versus what the company owes: assets versus liabilities. Unlike the income statement, which shows the amount of money that comes in the business versus the money that comes out, the balance sheet shows the wealth that the firm has accumulated over its lifetime, whether it is in physical forms like real estate or cash, or whether it is in financial assets like stocks and bonds. This is compared to the firm's debt. It is important to ensure that the debt is manageable. You want to make sure that the company will be able to pay off its debts because if it can't, the company will go bankrupt; they won't have any money left and the stock price will go to zero. In other words, if the company goes bankrupt since it has too much debt, you will lose all the money you invested. The best way to make sure debt is manageable is by using common sense. You do not want to invest in a company that has hundreds of millions of dollars of long term debt while the company is only making a few million dollars each year because the firm would never be able to pay it off. On the other hand, if the same firm has hundreds of millions of dollars of assets, firm would be able to liquidate the assets in order to pay off the debt, making it a safe investment. A good rule of thumb is to divide the total long term debt by the firm's free cash flow[9]. If this number is less than 3, then it is likely that it will be able to manage its debt.

It is also important to make sure that the firm can meet its short-term financial obligations; it must also be able to pay debts that are due soon. To do this, investors look at current assets and current liabilities. The word current is an adjective that means, in finance, "within one

---

[9] Free cash flow can be calculated by using data on the cash flow statement. It is calculated by subtracting the absolute value of capital expenditures from total operating cash flow.

year." Current assets are any assets that can be converted into cash within one year: cash, stocks and bonds. Current liabilities are debts that must be paid back within the next year. Many financial analysts will use the current ratio-current assets divided by current liabilities- in order to check whether the company has too much debt. Typically, it is alarming to investors if the ratio is less than one because it means that the firm does not have enough money to pay back debts that are due within the next year. If that company wants to keep operating, then they would need to borrow more money, increasing their debt burden. On the other hand, if the current ratio is at around 1.5, many investors would view this as healthy; the company has enough assets to pay off their debts. Thus, it is important for investors to check the balance sheet for current assets and current liabilities because if the investor fails to do so, the business he invests in might be in trouble.

It is also important to read the last of the three financial statements: the cash flow statement. This statement is often overlooked, but it provides valuable information to the investor. One of the first metrics to check for is the "total cash flow from operating activities." This number simply represents that amount of money that comes in the business versus how much goes out- just due to activities directly related to the core business model; this metric excludes income and expenses from income streams that are not related to the main way businesses make money. For example, investing activities would be excluded. Investors want to see this metric grow overtime because growth shows that the business is able to expand. Conversely, if the number is getting smaller each year, it either means that the business is bringing in less revenue or that its revenue is not coming from its main business. For example, Pepsi's (PEP) revenue could be increasing, even though they are not selling more soda, but because they are investing their money. If total revenue is increasing, but not cash flow from operating activities, it could signal that the main portion of the firm's business model is dying. Thus, it is important to look at the cash flow statement in order to make sure the business is still growing.

The Analysts

"Forecasts may tell you a great deal about the forecaster; they tell you nothing about the future."
-Warren Buffett

At the time I am writing this book, Warren Buffett has a net worth of over eighty billion dollars. He is the chief executive officer of Berkshire Hathaway (BRK.A), a conglomerate which he created. He is an icon in the investing community since he accumulated much of his wealth in the stock market. More specifically, he has made his money through value investing. Many people believe that he is one of the worlds smartest investors, and they are probably correct. Logically, many people buy what Buffett buys because he is a good investor. However, it is not a good decision to buy his stocks or to buy a stock because someone says it is good. Conversely, you should never sell a stock because someone sold their shares. Almost every beginner investor has thought about purchasing shares because an analyst recommended it. This chapter will explain why one should not make their purchasing decisions based off of analysts' decisions.

Many beginner investors who want to buy their first share of stock will make a decision by typing the following in Google: "Buy or sell stock XYZ." Then, hundreds of results will appear, all of which give a different opinion. So, the first problem with purchasing a stock based off of an analyst's opinion is that he could be flat out wrong.

There are so many opinions about a stock that it is impossible to know which one is correct. What made the beginner investor accept the opinion of one analyst over the other? In fact, many beginner investors will not even look beyond a couple of analysts' reports. Usually, only a few projections about a stock are correct; when a person buys shares based on another person's opinion, he is leaving his money at the chance that he clicked on the "correct" article. Even though some Wall Street analysts are correct at times, the wide range of opinions makes it risky to make a purchasing decision based off of one report because, in the long run, only a few will be correct. If only a few views are correct, how will a beginner investor know whether he read the correct article from a database that contains many viewpoints? It is also important to consider the intentions of many of these analysts.

Many, but not all, analysts do not look to provide genuine financial advice for the beginner investor; they are in it to make money. Many analysts work for a brokerage firm like Charles Schwab or Fidelity. Those firms make a $5 commission whenever someone trades a stock. That is how they make a profit. So, if no one were to trade stocks, the firm would not generate any revenue. It is important to consider that the firms want their analysts to spice up their reports. Some analysts might say that a stock should be sold off quickly before the price goes down in the short term, even though the analyst believes it is a good stock for the long term. They may spice up the report so people trade shares more often, thus generating more revenue for the brokerage. I would like to emphasize that they are not lying to investors, rather some of them are influenced to make it seem as if a buying opportunity is better than it really is or that they might exaggerate the flaws in a company in order to get more people to sell the stock. Once again, he probably truly believes that one should sell the stock, however, the analyst may exaggerate his claims.

A beginner investor should not make purchases based on analysts' opinions even if they do not work for a brokerage. Some analysts work for places like the Motley Fool, where the firm makes money based on the number of views they get on their articles. It is important to remember that some analysts may exaggerate their claims in order to gain attention and views. Thus, some analysts will exaggerate claims in order to get views, reducing the article's credibility.

A beginner investor should not buy stock based on analysts' opinions because everyone has a different risk tolerance. Since many analysts tend to have experience in the stock market, they tend to be older. You are probably asking what does age have to do with risk tolerance. Well, many older investors tend to be less risky with their money since they are coming close to retirement. On the other hand, many new investors tend to be young and can take more risk with their money since they do not need it in the short run. Thus, an analyst might recommend a stock that is not a risky investment while it might be better for the beginner investor to purchase more risky investments. This will hurt investors' overall performance because the growth rate will be significantly less.

I would like to emphasize that investors should not avoid reading analysts' report. Many of the analysts present data and statistics that can reveal whether a company is doing well or not. For example, an analyst discovered that Apple's (AAPL) iPhone sales growth was slowing down. Considering that iPhones make up a majority of the firm's revenue, the data that the analyst provides should be taken into consideration. However, his personal opinions about the company should not be taken into consideration. Some might say that it is fine since Apple's revenue is still growing while others might say that it is the end for Apple. At the end of the day, it is up to the beginner investor to use the facts presented by the analysts to make purchasing decisions. It is not optimal for an investor to use the analysts' opinions to make a purchasing decision because there are many opinions that can be derived from one fact. Thus, the beginner investor must make a distinguish fact and opinion when making purchasing decisions.

One of the main reasons why investors choose to pick individual stocks over other forms of investment like investing in the S&P 500 is to have control over their portfolio. The S&P 500 provides good and consistent gains but, many people do not invest in it since it does not give the investor control over what he invests in. However, when someone copies another person's stock picks, they are not achieving the control that is desired when one picks stocks individually. If one finds himself copying the portfolio of others, he should rather invest in a mutual fund that will handle all the transactions for him and provide him with a greater amount of diversity. Thus, it is best to not copy another investor's stock portfolio.

Diversification

"Diversify in stocks... as in much else, there is safety in numbers"
-Sir John Templeton

No matter what strategy an investor uses, he should always have a diversified portfolio. Diversification is when an investor mitigates risks by investing in different stocks, all of which have different characteristics.

Picture two situations in which both investors have ten thousand dollars in the market. In the first one, there is an investor who does not have a diversified portfolio. He has only invested in one company, 3m (mmm). If the company releases earnings and it does not meet expectations, the stock price may fall by 5%. He then loses $500 ($10,000*5%). On the other hand, in situation two, the investor has diversified across many companies. and 3m only makes up only 10% of his portfolio. The second investor's portfolio will only fall in value by $50 ($10,000*10%*5%). Since investor two spread his investments across many different stocks, he lost less money on a bad day. He was able to mitigate volatility and risk of his overall portfolio. Even Though 3m's stock fell in value, the second investor could have made money that day because his other stocks, making up 90% of the portfolio, could have made money and, it would have made up for the losses. The first investor, however, has guaranteed himself a loss since he has not diversified his portfolio. Thus, it is important to diversify in order to mitigate the risks of being reliant on one company; owning more companies allows an investor to spread the risk.

Now that the importance of diversification is apparent, we will discuss the ways an investor can diversify. A key misconception that many beginner investors have is that investing in many companies is diversification. In reality, that usually does not work because they typically do not diversify their portfolio in the correct way. Someone can still face similar results as investor number one unless he is conscious of the methods of diversification. In this chapter, the key learnings for a beginner investor are to learn the key methods of diversification.

An important way an investor can diversify is by investing in companies that operate in different sectors. If an investor buys shares in Apple (AAPL), Microsoft (MSFT), Micron Technologies (MU) and Nvidia (NVDA), he is not diversified. But why? This portfolio holds all tech-based companies. If the technology sector takes a hit, the investor's entire portfolio takes a hit. This is what we call diversification theatre. It is when an investor believes that he is diversified because he has invested in multiple companies. However, he is not diversified because all the companies operate in the same sector. A better portfolio would have involved investing in a tech company, an oil company, and a healthcare company. This set of stocks would have provided for greater protection from market volatility. Thus, it is essential for an investor to diversify across different sectors.

Another way for an investor to diversify is through dollar cost averaging. Dollar cost averaging is when an investor uses a set amount of money every month to purchase shares of stock no matter how the market is doing. It allows the investor to avoid investing a lump sum in the market at a bad time. If an investor purchases shares of Johnson and Johnson (JNJ) but, the next day the stock falls 10% due to an unforeseen problem with the company, the investor starts off with a 10% loss. That means the stock price has to rise by about 11% for the shareholder to break even. However, if the investor dollar cost averaged, and bought half of the shares initially and the half after the 10% decline, he would not need to recover 11% to break even. Since some of his shares were purchased at a lower price while some at the higher price, the shares that he purchased after the decline do not need to break even. Rather, the stock price needs to only rise by roughly 5% because the shares purchased after the decline would not be starting at a loss. Thus, dollar-cost averaging allows investors to diversify each of his holdings across a range of prices, mitigating the effects of entering a position at a bad time. Overall dollar-cost averaging is an excellent strategy for an investor to diversify his investments across time.

However, dollar-cost averaging is not perfect. First off, dollar cost averaging requires an investment on a periodic basis. Most investors dollar cost average on a monthly basis but, it can be done on almost any interval.

The investor only needs to be comfortable with it and, he must be consistent with it. However, whenever the investor dollar cost averages, he must always pay a commission; usually, it is $5. A small fee of $5 can be destructive to many beginner investors. If an average investor has $800 per month to invest in stocks and he currently has 4 positions, he can only devote $200 per stock. Assuming the commission is $4.95, the investor must receive a 2.5% gain just to break even. Over time, 2.5% will make a big difference in the return on investment. One way an investor can mitigate the effects of a commission is by investing in one stock each interval. This will allow the investor to invest the same amount of money and pay the commission only once; if he invests in 4 stocks in one interval, he will have to pay the commission 4 times. However, this will reduce the effect of dollar cost averaging. If an investor prolongs the interval, too much money might be invested at the wrong time. On the other hand, if an investor reduces the interval, he will be able to have a position at many different prices, instead of just a few, spreading the risk of a bad entry. Another way to lower the effect of a commission is by investing more money at a time. If a person invests more money, he needs a smaller gain per share in order to break even. However, this is not realistic in the short term for many beginner investors since it can take a long time to build up one's income. Nonetheless, there is a solution; reduce the commission. Although investors do not have control over the commission, they do have control over the brokerage firm they invest with. One brokerage firm, Robinhood, allows investors to purchase shares without commission. Only a few brokerages allow people to invest in stocks commission free, and Robinhood is the most prominent of them. The catch is that the stock researching capabilities are quite limited; however, this should not be an issue for the beginner investor because the information about corporations can be found on websites like yahoo finance. For a beginner investor, it is the best option to set up a Robinhood account so he can take advantage of not having to pay commissions in order to dollar cost average. Even though he will be invested with an "inferior" brokerage, it will allow him to make more money, which is really what matters at the end of the day. Therefore, beginner investors should open an account with Robinhood in order to create diversity in their portfolio.

However, when an investor dollar cost averages, it is important to remember the fundamentals of investing. As explained in the chapters called "The Logic of Value Investing" and "Cash is King: When to Buy a Stock," an investor should never purchase a stock while the price is high and expensive. Rather, he should purchase the stock at a discounted price that can be calculated by following the steps outlined in the chapter called "Cash is King: When to Buy a Stock." If an investor is dollar cost averaging, he never wants to buy it at a price above the Black Friday price. If he does, he will not be able to obtain a solid gain. Even if the investor already owns the stock, he does not want to purchase more shares above the sale price because that money could be used to buy shares in a company that is trading at its sale price. Also, a beginner investor should only use dollar cost averaging to decrease his cost basis[10]. For example, if a dollar-cost-averaging investor bought a stock that was at its sale price of $30, but, one month later, it is trading at a price of $25, he should buy more shares in order to lower the average cost of his investment. If he invested in a good company that is protected with a moat and has been increasing its profitability, the beginner investor will most definitely make his money in the long run, assuming he does not sell his shares early. By lowering his average total cost, his percent gain will increase because there would be a larger difference between the future stock price and average total cost. However, if the investor bought the stock when its price went from $30 to $40, which is no longer at the sale price, the investor would not be using his money efficiently because he could be buying stocks that are on sale. Also, by dollar cost averaging when the stock price is higher, he is increasing his cost basis, which will reduce his percent gain because there would be a small difference between the future stock price and the average total cost. Thus, an investor should only dollar cost average if the stock is still at or below its sale price and if it will lower the investor's cost basis.

---

[10] The word cost basis is a synonym for average cost per share and average total cost.

The ideal number of stocks

Diversification is a protection against ignorance.
  -Warren Buffett

In the modern investment world, there is no consensus on the number of stocks an investor should own. Some recommend owning only three stocks, while others advise that an investor should own forty to fifty stocks. Despite the lack of consensus, there is an ideal range for a beginner investor, and this chapter will identify the ideal range.

In order to determine the ideal number of stocks, we must compare the pros and cons of owning many or few stocks. Then, we must conclude which set of benefits and opportunity costs are best for a beginner investor.

First, we will explain the argument for owning many stocks. People who believe that an investor should own many stocks argue that when an investor owns many companies, he or she is more diversified and well protected from making a bad trade. For example, if someone owns two stocks, and one of the stock price collapses, the investor's overall portfolio value could fall dramatically. On the other hand, if the investor owned 50 stocks, and one of the stock prices collapsed, the investor would only lose a little bit of his total investment because his risk and money are spread across many different companies. Thus, some will contend that it is important to own many stocks because the diversification will reduce an investor's risk.

The view of owning about 50 stocks is commonly held by mutual fund[11] managers. These managers' views are biased because they want people to feel that it is necessary to own many stocks so that they buy a mutual fund as it is prohibitive to own 50 stocks, for an individual investor; most people cannot afford to pay the transaction cost of buying and selling 50 different stocks. Even with free trading brokers like Robinhood, it is difficult for many new investors to have the capital to purchase one share in 50 different companies. Many new investors also find it hard to name fifty different good companies which they understand and have researched. Due to general difficulty for an individual to own 50 stocks, many mutual fund managers persuade investors to purchase their index fund so that they make more money. Although they are usually genuine, it is still important to be aware that mutual fund managers are rewarded for advising people to own many stocks; if people believe that they need to own many companies and diversify their portfolio, they will buy shares of a mutual fund.

On the other hand, some investors recommend that people should own roughly three stocks, and Warren Buffett is an advocate for this. Investors like Buffett argue that when people over-diversify, their returns are small compared to if they had owned fewer companies. Historical

---

[11] A mutual fund is a type of fund that allows investors to pool their money in order to buy shares in firms that are picked by the mutual fund managers. These managers typically choose to own 40-50 stocks in their fund. The profits are divided among the investors.

evidence tends to support their assertion. Many individual investors who invest in a few handpicked stocks are able to beat the market over the long term. For example, investors like Warren Buffett and Charlie Munger usually outperform the market. Also, investors like Buffett claim that, when people invest in many companies, they are adding many bad ones to their portfolio. Investors like Buffett contend that, as investors invest in more companies *in order to diversify* their portfolio, they tend to invest in less attractive stocks because they feel obligated to invest in more companies, despite their valuation, thinking that it would help them. However, the investors' attempt to diversify their portfolio has actually lowered their returns because they are investing in overvalued firms; trying to diversify by adding more overvalued companies hurts the investor. According to Buffet, it does not make sense to overdiversify by investing in a good company and a bad company because the investor could have a larger return if he only invests in the good company. In order to maximize profits, one should invest in a few good companies, according to Buffett, rather than investing in many *good and bad* companies. Thus, investors like Buffett believe that an investor should invest in roughly three stocks in order to maximize profits; they maximize profits by reducing the number of bad investments.

However, similar to the institutional investors' strategy, Buffett's is not flawless. The main issue with minimal diversification for a beginner investor is that it can be risky because many beginner investors cannot perfectly distinguish a good stock from a bad stock. Buffett's strategy assumes that an investor can pick good stocks and distinguish them from the bad ones. However, beginner investors are not yet proficient at this skill, and they are still learning. Whenever someone learns a new skill, like picking stocks, he or she will not be proficient or effective at the beginning. It requires practice to get good at anything, like picking stocks.

After heeding to both sides of the diversification argument, it is clear that having minimal diversification is ideal for the experienced investor who can do due diligence and wants to maximize his or her profit. However, beginner investors are not experienced, and they need a "protection against ignorance," as in Buffett's terms, without losing the potential to yield large profits.

A beginner investor should invest in roughly five stocks only, if he is investing under $5,000. If the sum is split evenly across five companies, the investor would have a $1,000 stake in each company. By owning more than three stocks, the investor is able to have more room for error; if one of his stocks fell to $0, he would only lose a fifth of his portfolio, compared to a third when he was less diversified. Also, by owning five stocks, he is limiting the number of companies he invests in; he only invests in the ones that he can understand and has researched. By limiting the number of investments, he will naturally have less bad eggs in his basket as his best picks will most likely be good companies, if he does due diligence; there will be less room for bad companies in his portfolio to decrease his profits as an investor would naturally invest in his best choices first.

However, if the beginner investor has more than $5,000 to invest in the stock market, roughly nine stocks should be purchased for the same reasons mentioned above: it allows for sufficient diversification to prevent an error to wreck a portfolio, and it ensures that an investor is not over-diversifying, causing him to lose his profits to bad companies.

An investor should increase the number of stocks he should own with the amount of money he invests. As an investor increases the number of different stocks he owns, the commissions will increase and siphon an investor's profits; since he would naturally invest less money in each stock with each additional company he invests in, the investor would need a larger percent gain in order to break even due to the fixed commission. Thus, he must increase the amount of money he invests if the investor wants to own more companies, especially if he wants to avoid needing a large percent gain to break even. However, investors should set the limit at around nine stocks because owning too many will lead to over-diversification; he may start to invest in bad companies, causing him to lose some of his profits. However, nine, the maximum number of stocks an investor should own, is flexible. Investors can own a few more than nine stocks, or a few less than nine, depending on investor's characteristics: scope of knowledge and, dedication to investing.

The first characteristic, scope of knowledge, refers to the number of businesses the investor can understand. When an investor has a large scope of knowledge, he can easily understand many types of industries and businesses. Conversely, if an investor has a limited scope of knowledge, he can only understand a few particular businesses. When an investor has a comprehensive scope, he can naturally surpass the limit of nine without investing in bad stocks because he can understand more businesses and identify good ones. On the other hand, when an investor is limited in scope, he should invest in fewer firms because he can only understand the business models of a few. If he tries to invest in more stocks than he can understand, he will start to make poor investment decisions because his analysis will be weak; it would be like gambling because the investor would not be able to predict the outcome of a business he cannot understand. If he adds businesses he does not understand to his portfolio, he may be adding bad stocks and decreasing his return. Thus, the beginner investor should increase or decrease the number of stocks he owns, from the baseline of nine depending on his scope of knowledge.

The second characteristic that can determine the number of stocks an investor should own is his dedication to investing. An investor who is dedicated to investing, and has the time to research more companies can invest in more stocks as long as he does his research thoroughly. If an investor has the time to do proper research, he can successfully invest in more stocks. However, if the investor only has time to research five stocks, he should only invest in five stocks; he should not invest in a total of nine stocks because the other four that he did not thoroughly research would mitigate his returns; trying to diversify would hurt his returns because the risk would not be spread across good companies. Thus, an investor should adjust the number of stocks he owns so that it aligns with his commitment to investing.

Dividends

"Do you know the only thing that gives me pleasure? It's to see my dividends coming in."
- John D. Rockefeller

Dividends are a quarterly[12] payment that corporations pay to shareholders. In the past years, investors have been debating over whether a company pays a dividend or not is important in an investment decision: how important are dividends when we invest in stocks? In this chapter, we will explore the question by evaluating the pros and cons of investing in dividend-paying stocks.

The first con of investing in dividend paying stocks is the low growth potential. Most corporations that pay a dividend are well-established firms that have been operating for many years. This is because, in order to pay a dividend, the company needs to be financially stable. If a corporation is new and still growing, the company will most likely reinvest their profits because, at the beginning stages, they need cash in order to expand their business. Thus, the firms that pay a dividend are most likely not growing as fast and are just looking to sustain their business because they are already established firms; these companies are typically a dominant player in the industry. Since these companies are already established, they have a lower growth potential compared to that of a less

---

[12] The word quarterly means refers to a period of every 3 months because it is a quarter of one year.

established firm. Due to the lower growth potential of dividend-paying corporations, they will experience a smaller upside in their stock price; there will be a smaller chance for capital appreciation. Thus, non-dividend paying companies have bigger gains in their stock prices over the long run. Furthermore, when a company pays a dividend, they are taking profits right out of the company. In many dividend-paying stocks, it is about half of the company's net income. The money that is paid in dividends has a huge opportunity cost; the money that is paid out in the form of dividends cannot be used to grow and expand the business. The act of paying a dividend already hurts the company's potential to grow. This can hurt the company in the long run, causing a decline in their stock price. Thus, investing in dividend-paying companies can be bad as it correlates with lower capital appreciation and growth.

In spite of the cons of dividend-paying stocks, there are some pros. The first is that dividends provide a guaranteed source of income. Once a company announces that they will pay a dividend, they must legally make the payment to shareholders; a company cannot say they will pay a dividend and fail to do so. Therefore, a major benefit of a dividend is a guaranteed return. The guaranteed return is important for a couple of reasons.

Firstly, when the stock performs poorly, the dividend acts as a safety cushion for the investor. If the stock price declines 10%, a dividend can relieve some of the stress and make the actual loss only 8% or seven 7%. Even if the stock price is falling, the investor will gain some money due to the dividends. Thus, a dividend can relieve stress off of a declining stock price.

The next reason to invest in dividend stocks has to do with the nature of the company. As mentioned earlier, companies that pay a dividend are typically older and more established companies with lower growth potential. This is important because typically companies that pay dividends are blue chip companies[13] that have existed for a long time. Although this varies on a case by case basis, typically, a dividend signals that the company is in good financial health. Furthermore, dividend-paying companies tend to be stronger in business fundamentals. On the other hand, some, but not all, non-dividend-paying corporations tend to be riskier because those companies have not fully established themselves yet. It might mean that the firm is not in good financial health, or that it is not ready to pay a dividend. However, in general, dividend-paying companies are less prone to a business failure risk.

Pros	Cons
Stable Companies	Less Capital Appreciation
Guaranteed Return	

[13] A blue chip company is an adjective to describe a large company that is considered to be stable.

Well, here is the part every beginner investor wants to know; should I invest in dividend paying stocks? The answer for beginner investors is not straightforward. Many beginner investors in the stock market should be taking some risk as long as they are still quite young (under 40 years old) because young investors do not need the money they invest anytime soon; they need it to grow for the long run. Nonetheless, it is still good for a beginner investor's first stock to be a dividend-paying stock. But then why should they invest in dividend-paying stocks, which tend to be a safer investment? Typically, some new investors do not have enough discipline to adhere to all the principals in this book because they are too excited to enter the market. Typically, some new investors do not read the annual report or the balance sheet of the companies, nor do some of them have the patience to wait for a stock's price to come down because they want to start investing right away. Also, as mentioned earlier, it takes experience and practice to get good at any skill, so beginner investors may not be good at stock market investing at the start. In general, many new investors tend to be risky. This is why, for a beginner investor's first stock, he should invest in a company that pays a dividend; A dividend-paying stock will mitigate the risk that comes from the shortcomings of the beginner investor. The dividend will provide a safety cushion, and the stock will more likely be established and less volatile, preventing the new investor from panic selling. However, once the investor is more experienced, he should invest in a stock that may not necessarily pay a dividend in order to achieve higher growth rates. When a beginner investor becomes experienced and starts to invest in non-dividend-paying stocks, he should closely follow the advice in this book on when to buy a stock and how to know if a company is good because there will be no safety cushion, but there will be more risk.

When an investor is looking for a dividend-paying stocks, it is important to know the characteristics of a good dividend. One can do this by looking at the company's dividend history and metrics. The first metric to look at is the dividend yield. It represents the dividends per share divided by the price per share times one-hundred. It shows what percent of the share price will be received in dividends. A high dividend yield indicates that an investor will get more dividends per dollar he invests, while a low dividend yield will indicate that an investor will get less dividends for each dollar he invests. On Yahoo Finance, a good source for looking up information about a company, it is located under the summary page by the words "Forward Dividend and Yield." The number in the parentheses represents the dividend yield while the dollar value outside the parentheses represents the total dollar value of a dividend per share per year. Most investors will say that a good dividend yield is between two and five percent.

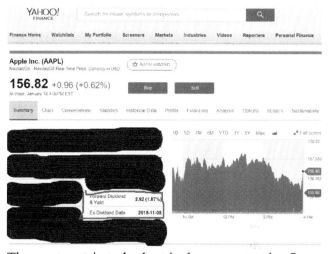

The next metric to look at is the payout ratio. On Yahoo Finance, it is all the way at the bottom of the statistics page. The payout ratio is calculated by dividing the total cash paid out in dividends by the net income times one-hundred. It shows what percent of the firm's net income is being paid out in dividends. The optimal percentage depends on the investor's goals. If the investor is looking for a company that will grow its dividend in the future and, if he expects to hold the stock for the long term, which he should, then the investor should aim for a payout ratio of around 40%-60%. Anything below that and the company is only paying a small percentage of their income to shareholders; there are many other stocks where investors can get a higher dividend. If the payout ratio is above 60%, the company is less likely to increase its dividend in the future because it still needs some capital to continue operations; the dividend has little room to grow. However, this is not necessarily a bad thing. Some experienced investors who are approaching retirement will look for slow-growing companies that pay out most of their income in dividends because it allows an investor to make a large, steady stream of passive income. If someone is looking for companies that already are paying out most of their money in dividends, the investor should look for a payout ratio between 50% and 70%. If the payout ratio starts to surpass 80%, the company might start not to make enough profit to continue operations. The company will look to cut its future dividend which is terrible for investors; not only will the investors receive fewer dividends but the stock price will decline and, investors will suffer some losses.

The next step is to make sure that the company has been able to sustain a growing dividend in the past. On Yahoo Finance, if the investor clicks on the historical data tab and then on "Show Dividends Only" and then extends the frequency to the past twenty years, he will see the company's dividend history. There are a few things to check for under the dividend history tab. The first is to check for how long the company has been paying a dividend for. There is not an exact number but beginner investors should look for a company that has been paying a dividend for at least the past five years because it shows that the firm is willing to pay dividends in the future; if the firm has only paid dividends for two quarters, it is unclear if the firm will pay dividends in the upcoming years because they lack a track record. The investor should also check if the dividend is growing. If the investor looks at the dividend payment for each quarter, he should optimistically see that the dividend payout is increasing over time and that there is never a time of a declining dividend payment or a time period where the company stopped paying the dividend. When analyzing the dividend history, the investor should not look at years 2008 and 2000 because, during those times, many companies' dividends were affected by the .com bubble and the 2008 financial crisis. So, if a company cut their dividend in 2008 or 2000, the investor should not worry at all or take that into account because many dividends were cut so that the firms could stay in business. Therefore, when investors look at the company's dividend track record, they should look for a dividend that has been rising over a long period of time, without taking into account the dividend cuts of 2000 and 2008.

The last way to check if a company's dividend is good is by looking into their financial health. It is crucial to look at a company's financial health because it will determine whether its dividend will be sustainable in the future. If the overall financial health is declining, it can be a signal that the firm will be unable to sustain its current dividend and that they will need to cut it in the future. There are three types of financial statements to look at when determining the firm's financial health: income statement, balance sheet, and the cash flow statement.

The key thing to look at on the company's income statement is the net income. When looking at net income, there is not a specific number that is good or bad since it is all relative to the size of the business and industry. Rather, it is more important to look at the company's revenue compared to past years. Beginner investors want the net income to be increasing over the years, or at least to be stable over the years. If the firm has one or two bad years but then recovers, their dividend will most likely be sustainable. A red flag would be if the net income is continually falling. If the net income is falling, the dividend will eventually eat too much of the net income, creating a high payout ratio and forcing the company to cut the dividend.

The next statement to look at is the balance sheet. Balance sheets show the debts and assets of a company. The most important metric on the balance sheet is the long term debt. The long term debt shows how much money the company owes to creditors in a year or longer. Just like the net income metric, there is no magic number because all the numbers are relative to the industry and the size of the firm. However, in order to see if a dividend is sustainable, the investor should make sure that too much debt is not being accumulated; if the firm has too much debt, it will not have enough cash flow to pay the dividends. In a best-case scenario, the long term debt would be decreasing over the years. But, that is not always true for a good stock that pays a dividend; in many cases, the debt is increasing. To make sure that the company is able to pay it off, the investor can look at the "cash flow from operating activities." This metric shows how much money is coming in or out of the business from everyday activities (if the number is positive, more money is coming into the business, and if the number is negative[14], more money is leaving the business). As long as the debt divided by the cash flow from operating activities is less than 33%, most investors would consider the debt to be manageable. Thus, as long as the debt to cash flow from operating activities is less than 33%, the firm's debt should not impact its ability to pay out dividends.

Before we conclude the chapter on dividends, we must discuss the dangerous dividend trap. It is when a corporation appears to be paying out a lot of dividends because the yield is high, even though it is not sustainable. Although a high dividend yield is hard to ignore, in reality, the yield is not high because the company is paying a lot of dividends. Rather, it is high because the firm's stock price has been declining in recent years. Remember that the dividend yield is calculated by dividing the dividend per share by the price per share. If the price per share starts to fall because the company is starting to fail, the dividend yield will increase. However, many beginner investors will not notice this, and they will invest in the company because they think it is super successful due to the high yield. In reality, the investor has bought shares in a company that is struggling. In order to avoid this, the investor should be alerted when he sees an unusually high dividend yield, and

---

[14] On financial statements, a negative number is usually represented by parentheses. So, if the company lost $300 in net income, it would appear on the balance sheet as "($300)."

he should look to see why the yield is so high. A good way to find out if a company has been struggling is by reading an article on it by an analyst[15]. Thus, beginner investors need to figure out why a company's dividend yield is so high in order to avoid a dividend trap.

---

[15] Remember that reading an analysis article is not always bad. In fact, most analysts provide key metrics and information that investors should know about a company. Rather, it is bad for an investor to purchase shares of stock because someone thinks it is a good buy.

Speculative Stocks

"The individual investor should act consistently as an investor and not as a speculator."
  - Benjamin Graham

Speculative stocks should be avoided by all long term investors because of their unpredictability that makes it difficult to determine an attractive price to pay for its shares.

Although there are many types of speculative stocks, the general definition of a speculative stock is any business that has unpredictable, future profitability.

Speculative stocks are dangerous to invest in for long-run investors. When an investor does not have certainty about a firm's future profits, there is little certainty about a return on investment; if future profits are not certain, a return on investment is not certain. Would you buy all the shares of a company for $1 billion if the firm only had a 10% chance of returning your $1 billion? Every sensible investor would not purchase those shares because there is a small chance of making money. The same logic applies to purchasing a portion of a company; an investor should not purchase a company if it is uncertain to generate a reasonable amount of cash flow.

If speculative stocks are so risky, why do investors purchase them? Well, with speculative stocks especially, the upside of a potential investment tends to be large with a speculative stock. So, many investors decide to take the risk of investing in speculative stocks, even though it is similar to gambling. With speculative stocks, there is a small chance to double or even quadruple one's investment. However, there is a large chance that he will lose most of his investment. Some investors decide to gamble with speculative stocks, and their results are never predictable. Since intelligent, beginner investors want to avoid large risks, they should avoid speculative stocks due to its risky nature.

There are many ways an investor can invest in speculative stocks, and this chapter will focus on the main types of speculative stocks so that a beginner investor can avoid these types of companies.

The first type of speculative stock is a commodity stock. A commodity is any product that is identical across the entire industry, and the price of the product is completely determined by supply and demand. For example, there is no difference between gold bought from Lear Capital and the Hartford Gold Group; the products are identical. Also, the price the firms charge is determined by supply and demand; Lear Capital cannot charge more money for its gold because consumers can just go purchase the same gold from the Hartford Gold Group, as long as they sell it at the market price. The only way Lear Capital can charge more money is if there is a smaller supply of gold or greater demand for gold. However, even if Lear Capital can charge more money for the gold, so can the Hartford Gold Group; both firms charge the same price for the commodity. Commodity stocks' revenue is thus based on market conditions- supply and demand. These firms make more money when the demand of their commodity is high and less when the demand is low. The most popular commodity stocks tend to be involved in the sale of natural resources and standardized goods like steel, coal, wood, and iron.

Commodity stocks' profits are unpredictable because the price of their product is unpredictable. There is almost no one who can predict the price of a commodity in the long run because there are many unforeseen factors that can affect the supply and demand such as technological changes, number of competitors, input costs, producer price expectations, fiscal policy, expected population growth, consumer preferences, and the price of substitutable and complementary goods. If an investor calculated how the endless list of determinants will affect the commodity, he must then calculate the magnitude of the determinants. This task is physically impossible for beginning investor because no one can foresee into the future to such an extent, creating an unpredictable price for the business and return on investment for the investor.

The unpredictable nature has led to volatile profits for commodity stocks which is mirrored by a volatile and an unpredictable market capitalization. For example, the AK Steel Holding Corporation (AKS) was losing over $500 million per year in 2015, when steel prices were low, relative to its future price. However, as the price of steel rose due to unpredictable factors during 2017, the AK Steel Holding Corporation was able to make over $100 million in profits by the end of 2017. This is correlated with a rise in their stock price; it rises from $2 per share in 2015 to over $10 per share in 2017. The supply and demand changes in the steel industry have allowed the firm and investors to make money. However, their gains were unpredictable, and there was an equal chance that the investors would have lost their money due to changes in supply and demand. Hence, the unpredictable correlation between market conditions and commodity stocks' success makes them a risky and speculative investment.

Price of Steel

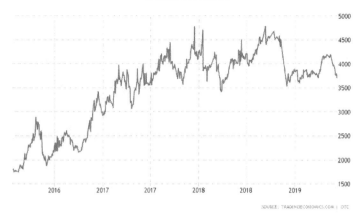

AK Steel Holding Corporation's Stock Price

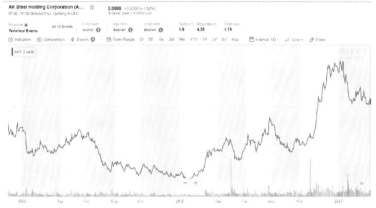

The second type of speculative stock occurs when the firm's cash flow does not justify its valuation. In other words, this is when a firm makes little profit, or even loses money, but the stock still trades at a high valuation. These speculative investments rely on the fact that, one day, the firm will experience massive growth in order to have large profits each year, allowing investors to see its stock price rise by 40%, 60%, 100%, or even 300%. Although the reward is large, so is the risk with speculative stocks that currently do not make money.

The main issue with companies that cannot currently make money is that they lack predictability with future returns because those firms do not have a proof of concept. A proof of concept is evidence that proves a business concept is feasible and profitable in the market. For example, if an investor wants to invest in a new tech start-up, he would look to see if the firm is able to make money. If the firm shows that it has sold their software to many people in the region, the investor would be able to decide whether the firm's profitability justifies its valuation. However, if the firm has not sold any software yet, the investor has no way to determine or predict the firm's profitability, making it hard to decide on its valuation or fair price to pay; if you were opening a business and could not roughly predict your profits for the next month, you would not know your maximum willingness to spend on costs for that month either. The same logic applies to an investor. If he cannot determine how much money the business will return for him, he cannot determine the price to pay for the business. When he buys a stock that lacks a proof of concept, he is likely to overpay because the current valuation doesn't justify its current ability to generate cash.

The most controversial example of a speculative stock that cannot currently generate a sufficient profit is Tesla (TSLA). Tesla, a $40 billion company, is a firm that is currently one of the industry leaders in producing electric cars. It is known for producing autonomous vehicles and for being a high-end brand. Despite its feats, its finances are quite weak; the firm is unable to consistently make a profit, and the firm usually loses money. Tesla lost over $1 billion in 2017, and there is little evidence that it will be able to change the situation anytime soon. If an investor were to purchase the entire company for $40 billion, he would lose about $1 billion per year. This decision is irrational unless there is clear evidence of improved profitability for the firm. Therefore, Tesla would be a speculative investment because its future return is unpredictable, making it nearly impossible to determine a discounted price to pay for its shares. In conclusion, an investor should always avoid commodity and low-income stocks because they are not predictable in their future profits, making it risky to determine a fair price to pay for their shares.

When to Sell a Stock

"The right time to sell a company is never."
-Warren Buffett

The last step for an investor to claim his gains is to sell his stock. Assuming that the investor followed the previous steps correctly, the investor will almost be guaranteed a large gain. However, the investor needs to decide when to sell the stock in order to maximize his profit. An investor wants to avoid selling a stock too early or too late because it will not allow him to maximize his gains. For long-term investors who look at business fundamentals, there are only a few cases in which they should sell their shares: the business model changes, the business becomes financially unstable, or if the market price is above the fair price.

The first reason to sell one's shares is if the business model changes. The business model is the way the business operates: the customer the firm targets, the way the firm makes money, the products the firm sells. When the firm changes a significant portion of its business model, an investor should consider whether the business is still worthy to invest in because the changes may make it less profitable. For example, in 2014, Amazon was an online store and that is about it. However, in 2017 and 2018, it made significant changes to its business model. The firm added many new services and business segments: Kindle Direct Publishing, Amazon Web Services, Whole Foods, and smart stores. Anyone who owned Amazon's stock before these additions and changes must consider whether the company is still worth owning because the changes could make the firm weaker. For example, when Amazon decided to buy Whole Foods, some investors were concerned that Amazon made a poor decision by investing in physical stores because many people believe that they were dying out. Considering that Whole Foods represents a significant portion of Amazon's expenses, some investors might have sold their shares. Thus, an investor might want to sell his shares of stock if the firm makes significant, adverse changes to the business model.

Investors should also look for adverse business trends when deciding to sell a stock. This means, if a company starts to show signs of failure, the investor should sell his shares because it is likely that the share price will fall along with the business. There are multiple indicators when looking for unfavorable trends.

One of the most important trends to look for is the slow death of an industry. The best example of a company that is experiencing a slow death is Barnes and Noble (BKS)- a major player in the book industry. In the early 2000s, ebook started to become popular among everyday readers. Consequently, readers read less from physical books, leading to less sales for Barnes and Noble. The decline of the physical book industry was paralleled with a decline in Barnes and Noble stock price. On April 1, 2010, the firm's stock price was at $14.46. At this time, some investors realized that ebooks are going to take over, and they sold their shares. However, some did not pay attention to the macro-industry trend, and they decided to hold their shares. Due to their lack of awareness of the industry trends, they had to take major losses. During April of 2019, the stock price was around $5.10; negligent investors lost over 60% of their investment because they did not realize that ebooks were trending. Thus, it is important for investors to look at industry trends.

Investors should also look at financial trends when determining when to sell a business. Unlike when one looks to purchase a stock, investors want to look for declining revenues and profits on the income statement as signals to sell the stock. Investors want to sell the stock if the profits are falling because it could signal the decline of the company. Assuming that an investor purchased his shares in a company while its net income and revenue were increasing, he has most likely made a sufficient return on investment. As long as the company is still growing, the investor should not sell his shares because the value of those shares would most likely rise in value. On the other hand, if the firm starts to see their profits fall, it could signal that the company will start to decline. Then, the investor should sell his or her shares because, over time, the company will become less valuable. The best example of a large firm that started to fail is General Electric (GE), a conglomerate[16]. Throughout 2016, General Electric made

---

[16] A conglomerate is a common word that describes the industry a company operates in, It is used to describe a company that operates in many industries. They use this word instead of listing each industry the company operates in.

about six billion dollars in net income. Although this statistic might make the company seem like a good investment, it was on a downward trend. In 2017, the company lost eight billion dollars and in 2018, it lost twenty billion dollars. If an investor recognized that the firm's profits were declining, he could have avoided large losses; from 2016 to 2018, the stock price collapsed by over 65%. Thus, an investor should look at financial trends in order to look for warning signs when deciding to sell a stock.

The last reason an investor should sell his shares occurs when the market price of a stock is above the stock's fair value. Remember, the fair value of a stock is equal to its future value divided by four (review the end of the chapter called *Cash is King: When to Buy a Stock* for a more in-depth review on the calculation). If an investor owns a stock when the market price is above its fair value and continues to hold it, he will not achieve his annual goal of an average 15% gain because the stock price is likely overvalued, which would cause it to fall. Moreover, if the investor owns the stock when it is trading above its fair value, he would have a severe opportunity cost because he could be invested in stocks that are deeply discounted instead of overpriced; by investing in discounted stocks, he would have a larger long-term gain. Thus, an investor should sell his shares if the market price is above its fair value.

If none of the three selling situations- the business is no longer stable, the business model significantly changes, the market price exceeds the fair price- occur, then the intelligent investor should hold his shares because the stock would be trading below its intrinsic value, assuming the investment was not made in a speculative company and the research was thoroughly completed by the intelligent investor. When a stock is trading below its intrinsic value, it is discounted, allowing investors to make a near-guaranteed profit. Therefore, unless one of the conditions occur, the beginner investor should not sell his shares because it will most certainly increase in value because it is trading below its intrinsic value.

Now that you have finished the book, you have the knowledge to make incredible gains in the stock market. Therefore, you are no longer a beginner investor, but an intelligent investor. The next step is clear: start investing!

About the Author

Danial Jiwani is a 17 years old high school senior. He is passionate about stock market investing. He has spent the last couple of years learning about the strategies successful investors use to beat the stock market at its own game. Currently, he is one of the youngest authors who write books about business. Danial has also taught many students about microeconomics in his book called *Surviving AP Econ: Microeconomics.* Through his books, Danial is always sharing knowledge with the youth of the world.

Printed in Great Britain
by Amazon

33457142R00064